Red Clay Scholar

The Journey

Ironbutt

PublishAmerica
Baltimore

First printing

PublishAmerica has allowed this work to remain exactly as the author intended, verbatim, without editorial input.

Hardcover 978-1-4560-5718-3
Softcover 978-1-4560-5717-6
PUBLISHED BY PUBLISHAMERICA, LLLP
www.publishamerica.com
Baltimore

Printed in the United States of America

Everyone has a Story,
Everyone has a Journey.
This one is mine.
Enjoy.

NorButt 9/17/2012

A Collision of Fate

By Ironbutt
Written with no rules or format;

He was a loner, destined to forever not run with his kind. Part wolf, part dog. Feared by some. Respected by others but never accepted. Destined to roam alone.

She was an aspiring writer, forever jotting down notes. A slave to her laptop. Waiting and searching for that eye catching happening. Something she could make the world see through her eyes as put to pen.

He slowly made his way down toward the village. Caution at every turn. The last encounter with the village dogs had not been a good one. The farmer, yes the farmer, his haste to shoot at anything moving had saved him that time. May not be so lucky again. So he moved with caution. He could smell the people. Their waste. Their bodies. The dog in him longed to smell this forever. The wolf in him regarded it with distain.

She was busy as ever in her car. One hand on the wheel the other reaching for a pad and searching for her pen. She knocked over her soft drink on to the paper. Damn! She momentarily let go of the steering wheel to recover the damage. The damage, right!

He had made it to the center of the road when the unexpected lights covered his dark body. He tried to evade but the humans vehicle was out of control. Pain! More pain.

He woke up with his left paw mangled. He tried to yelp out in pain but his jaw wouldn't move yet he was alive. Alive and breathing. He moved slowly off the road and then...the dog in him sensed something wrong. The wolf in him picked up the smell of blood and a faint human voice.

He moved to both.

She had been thrown clear of the vehicle. The seat belt that would have saved her from injuries, she had undone to recover the spilled drink. Her vehicle was a total, lying on its side with all the belongings scattered in the field. She couldn't see. The concussion had blinded her.

Her left leg was useless. She was unable to move, and then she sensed something. Something huge!

He slowly circled the carnage, the smell of blood driving him insane...the sense of a human in need causing an internal struggle. He closed in, inches away from her. Something was wrong with this human; she wasn't throwing things at him or yelling, he was confused. Suddenly his confusion was stopped with the humans hands on his mane. The wolf in him wanted to bolt but the dog in him welcomed the touch. The touch missed from so many years ago. A rush of memories flooded his clouded head. He lay down beside her. Why he didn't know, almost instinct.

She had sensed his presence. She could smell him. Feel him yet she could still not see. Felt his hot breath on her. A dog! Oh thank God, you sent me a dog to keep the wolves away until help arrives. Thank you. She ran her fingers through his mane, comfort to know he was there. A buzz near her left hand alerted her that her cell phone was closer then she thought. Again thank you Lord. She fumbled with the buttons and dialed 911. Help would be close by.

He heard the sirens, knew what they meant. Saw the vehicle come down the road, stop and watched as humans came running toward them. He stayed as long as his wolf sense would let him, then he darted into the undergrowth. He could hear them talking excitedly. Could tell that she was trying to get them to do something.

She kept asking them to take the dog too but they only figured she was under shock. They moved her into the vehicle and shut the doors. They were gone.

He moved to where she had laid, circled and laid down on the warm spot. Alone again.

A Father's Advice

By Ironbutt

My Daughter once felt bad about failing at
something. This was my advice to her.

If we treat life as a race, we could clearly see,
winners can come from the back of the pack and
suddenly take the lead.
As long as you're in the race you have won all
along.
It is when you don't try to keep going that you
start going wrong.
The leader of the pack will change throughout the
race.
Some will give it too much and soon lose the pace.
As long as you can see someone's back, you're
still hanging in,
one foot in front of the other increases the chance
to win.
Even if the victory flag eludes your grasp this
time,
you have done more by trying then those on the
sidelines.
Everyday a new runner will step up to set the
pace.
Accept the challenge of a new day...who knows...
today could be your day!

A Veterans Tribute;
For the People Sent Him Away

See not with your eyes...for the eyes see not all.

And it came to past that the People cried out for a warrior.

One who will mount the mighty war horse, wield the sword of thunder

And wear the armor of the People.

There came a visitor to the town yet he wore no Armor. Carried no sword and rode not his mighty stead.

Rather he had bundled up his armor, for he came not for war but for peace and hope.

He rode not his mighty stead, for it too had suffered and was looking forward to

Pulling the plow, that would prepare the land, ready for the seeds of peace.

The People were disappointed and sent them both away!

As the young warrior passed the outskirts of town a crippled man stopped them both.

Not crippled from age or disease but the agonies of too many wars.

"Come, here you will rest and plant your seeds of peace. Use my land, for peace has to start somewhere and the healing may start at the first sign of sprouting."

Sometimes it takes someone who has been on the Journey to understand the Journey. Thank a Vet.

A Long Talk

By Ironbutt

I did a sit down with my guardian angel the other
night, said, look I got this question, right.
Where is it that I am heading, am I even going
right?
Course by some divine pact made long ago up
above,
he really on that subject couldn't talk.
So I tried it a different way,
said, if I keep going the way I am now,
will I make it to the big town.
Ah, he was a bright one, that Angel, sent to me
for all these years.
Said he with a little grin,
its hard keeping up with you, and all these places
we have been.
I have always made sure you would never fall
but I do enjoy watching every now and then you
hitting the wall.
This makes you the man that you are and always
will be,
now quite asking all these questions and get some
sleep.
Smile
Ironbutt. Turn the Page

A Memorial: Do I Trouble You?
By Ironbutt

Do I trouble you... a white cross on this field?
Do I trouble you.... a pair of boots, weapon and a
helmet of steel?
Do I trouble you...men and women weep openly
without shame.
Do I trouble you? Do I? I will ask you once again.
Do I trouble you... flags will hang at half mast
today,
flowers and ribbons even a parade.
Young and old alike will have something to
share...you see,
a grim reminder, a promise....Freedom is not free!

A Small Town: On a Lighter Note
By Ironbutt

Got Copenhagen cans and a stained spit cup,
Pass with Care sticker on my truck.
Was born and raised right over there,
know a little bit about everything that goes on
around here.
It is a small town.
Like what's Her Name and You Know who
got caught the other day in a hotel room.
Now that's the news that don't make the paper,
gives a whole new meaning to love they neighbor!
It is a small town.
Heard Old Bobby's prize bull got loose,
messed up the garden belonging to Mary Ann
Lou,
she's the kind of woman won't stand still,
took out the double barrel and that bull got killed!
Now both of them are mad but they'll work it out,
sounds like a mess of collards and a surprise
cookout!
It is a small town.

A Tribute;
Women are Veterans Too
By Ironbutt

Yes I served with my Brothers and my pride rings through
but I'd be less of a man if I forgot my Sisters too.
White knuckles on a weapon held,
they too faced the fury of combats Hell.
Tears on their faces and blood on their hands,
they still held the line like any other man.
So the next time you cheer and want to buy a cold brew,
remember in combat...Bullets don't choose.
So pass that beer to the Lady my Man,
you are in the presence of a Veteran!

Abuse

By Ironbutt

I know you have been abused; I have driven by
you several times.
Seen you at the corner of the house, alone, dirty,
neglected.
It turns my stomach to see you this way, makes
me want to just take a shake some sense into
him. Show him how beautiful you are and not
abuse you so.
I hear him talking trash about you .How you
cannot cut it anymore and how he should have
never gotten you in the first place.
Then I got the call.
Seems he did leave you, oh happy day! Now I can
see you, run my fingers across your abused body
and bring life back to you.
Excitement runs through my veins as I pull up in
the yard. Oh no...
You're not where I usually see you! Did I pull up
at a bad time?
What's this? A new man comes to greet me? That
was quick!
Ah, but it is alright. I knew you wouldn't be alone
long, not you.
There is something different about this one
though, he cares, shows compassion.
He is asking a lot of questions about you. I feel
awkward answering them. More shocked am I
that he is willing to leave us alone together, just

you and me and ....this tool box.
So...come on Baby let's get you running and
sounding like new! There is grass that needs
cutting!
Smile

Airborne

By Ironbutt

We are Airborne Soldiers and we ride the
midnight skies.
When freedom is in jeopardy, we bring liberation
from up high.
We know the risk we are taking, some of us will
fall,
Airborne Soldiers, forever answering the call.
We come from a long line of traditions
dated back to WW11,
our resolve is still as strong now as the day we
said I do.
To be an Airborne Soldier takes more than the
best.
Airborne Soldiers...Silver Wings upon their chest.
We've held the frozen grounds, desert waste land
and the jungle floor.
We've given our share of blood for freedoms sweet
rewards.
Our ranks are replenished with brave men and
women too.
Stepping up for the of call of freedom...Sky
Soldiers here for you.

Alert

By Ironbutt

Somehow there is a thief afoot in the Land Of
Dreams,
quick, I think something should be done, call the
authority.
Alert the security, have them mount a search.
There will be no rest tonight; we must be on a
high alert.
Once the thief finds the chest, the chest where we
store Hope,
all our dreams will be for not, oh this cannot go
on.
The Lights of Wisdom cut through the fog,
the fog that clouds our mind.
It is the highest priority, this thief we must find.
Security of the Land of Dreams must never, ever
be breached.
Without the sprig of Hope, our Dreams will never
be.
Ah, there is the trumpet blare, the search is now
complete.
The thief is locked away, we rest with security.
Tonight, here in Dream Land, we all can come
and rest.
Lay gentle heads upon our sheets; let Hope do its
best.
Dare to dream, the dream of love, money or
anything.

For as long as Hope is secured, the possibilities it can bring.

Always on my Mind

By Ironbutt

As I ride my scoot my mind is on a roll.
From the job I just left to the bills I owe.
Still an uncompleted grocery list,
laundry that needs doing to a call I missed.
Engine rumbles under neath my butt;
realize I need to work on my clutch.
Need to remember not to forget ...
ah hell what was that, I need to start making a
list.
Ok diapers it was on the way home,
still need to figure out how to pay on the phone.
Stomach starts making a familiar sound,
can't remember if I laid the pork chops out.
Wind goes whistling past my ears,
better slow down, there are cops out here.
Mind goes on faster than this bike;
hope it will give me a break tonight.

Angels among Us

By Ironbutt

There are angels among us, no wings will you see.
Patient watching guardians, calming the seas.
You will find them in a soup line, coffee cup in
hand,
warming a chilled person, helping to understand.
I once met an angel in a faraway place,
I had lost all hope for comfort, was filled with
rage.
With a touch of her wings, I found the strength to
go on,
calming the fury, my frustration was gone.
Bullets fell around me, like a shield you could not
see;
I finished my mission, the angel right beside me.
There are angels among us, their wings you might
not see,
patient watchers, guardian of the peace.

Beneath

By Ironbutt

Here I am sucked into this abyss.
Signs of life above me that I will miss.
To struggle is useless, motionless I remain,
and the shackles of worries bring on the pain.
Again I see a shimmer of light,
focus, focus...Just one try.
It feels that I am moving, maybe try again.
I have to be moving, there is that light again.
The coldness of the abyss is exchanged with
warmth.
I awake to my pains, shut off the alarm.
The echoes of my flip flops as I walk down the
hall,
remind me I am still alive, Hello World Bring it
On!

Betrayal

By Ironbutt

The arrow of betrayal pierces my chest,
I stumble, fall, lay here my final rest.
The arrow is not shot from enemy unknown...
the fingers on the string belong to someone I
know.
Only you could have gotten this close with my
guard
laid aside....
my vision fades with you in my eyes.
Alas, I hope for you this victory is sweet,
for no other could accomplish this betrayal feat.
When the winds blow in the morn, my soul will
take flight....
my mind will take comfort...I 'vet done all for the
right?
I will join the angels that have protected the
weak...
you will find the demons; I tried so hard from you
to keep.

Brande's Song

By Ironbutt

She could barely reach that fountain,
determination on her face.
Steady pushing on that button, water splashing
all over the place.
High on her Barney sneakers, she finally got that
drink,
it was times like that, makes me stop and think.
I realize...I've been blessed.

Cause the world wasn't right when she came on
this earth.
I could have walked away from hundreds of hurts.
But we stuck it through and we got it right...
I get my kiss in the evening and a Daddy
goodnight.

Tied a pillow to her bottom, she's got her Barbie
helmet on,
going to try out those new skates, worry she don't
fall.
Skinned our knees and an elbow, finally got it
right.
She is out there skating, what a beautiful sight.
I realize...I've been blessed.

She packs her little suit case. Got her mp3 player
on.
Lost in her own world, singing to every song.

It's her Mammas turn this weekend and I got to play along,
she calls me when she gets there saying "Daddy it won't be long"
and I realize ...I've been blessed.

Cause the world wasn't right when she came to this earth.
I could have walked away from hundreds of hurts.
But we stuck it through and we got it right...I get a kiss in the evening
and a Daddy Goodnight.

We've moved on from skates and Barbie, she wants to get a car,
worked hard this summer and saved her money in a jar.
I made that girl a promise, I would go in half.
So we're looking in the paper and answering an ad
as I watch her now, I realize....I've been blessed.

Butterfly wings and Melodies
By Ironbutt

It's been awhile since the Barney tunes rung in
my head the whole day through.
That reminds me of a song, the joke of the day.
I wasn't the only parent that felt that way.
Dismantled Barbie and squeaky toys.
Bubble baths and diaper loads.
Oh how I relaxed when they all turned eighteen,
now my silence is interrupted it seems.
Congrates all around, you're a Grandpa,
no more midafternoon naps out in the lawn.
Time to childproof the house one more time,
put up all the little knickknacks young hands
seem to find.
I am so excited I can barely stand;
it's a young girl you know...here we go again!
They say that I will spoil this one just like the
rest.
Give her the shirt of my back so she can have a
dancing dress.
Well I say I am guilty and have been all along,
just sounds damn funny, me... a Grandpa!

Chili: Food only for Lovers
By Ironbutt

Yep the temp was a dipping down
and the chill was nipping the bones.
So the best way to get it right
was a homemade chili bowl.
Now there is a thing or two you need to know
when that chili settles down.
You've got to be with the one you love
when that chili wants to come out.
Aint no real way to explain the fact,
aint no need to say you won't.
Be you man or lady fair,
that chili gets you going.
So just fill that bowl up to the top
grab some onion and some cheese
and when that chili gets to working
just walk out into the breeze!

Choices

By Ironbutt

We all make choices; we have to live with the rest
of our lives.
In combat I made choices, prayed to God that I
was right.
I admit I stumbled between a woman and a wife,
the choice I made back then changed the course
of my life.
We argue in front of the children, not aware that
they can hear,
the choices we are making will ring in their ears.
It seems so hypocritical to tell them to things
right,
when we made bad choices right in front of their
eyes.
When we make these choices, be aware that there
is someone,
we all cannot have the rainbows, somewhere rain
has to fall.
My life has been a journey, recorded on my back,
now I'm left with choices, there is no looking
back.
Will she remember the reason she is here.
Will she remember our journey that has brought
us here?
Yes the taste of freedom is right there on her
tongue,
yet the choice she is about to make here, will
never be undone.

Dancing Bloomers on Parade
By Ironbutt

Now I remember way, way back, when I was a kid,
Granny's washed bloomers were always hid.
Either in the washroom, or shower stall,
or next to the heater down the hall.
Now driving through the country I behold,
folks have given up that practice of long ago.
There on the line, in bold display,
we got wind dancing bloomers on parade!
Now some are held captive with at least,
six to ten clothes pins I can see.
Some are colorful, look at me.
Some aint as new as they use to be!
Some makes me wonder about the lady of the house,
others just hang there, quite, glad to be out.
Well all in all, it's an art to see,
dancing bloomers just out in the breeze!

Darkness

By Ironbutt

Uncompromising, unyielding.... the mighty oak
snaps.
So cold, numb, confused...the fowl of summer
take flight.
Alone, tired, red eye shut to the morning glare....
 Mind is numb....
 is it I?
 Clock still ticking...time has not stood still.
Reality sinks in on what is now and what has
been.
 Mind is reeling from the truth.
 It is I. I, me, the one....
 The one who realizes the damage done
once again to the heart. The one organ that seems
to be working overtime.
 Snap. Just fricken snap and get it over with!
Don't compromise...don't find an excuse. Just
fricken SNAP!
 It is I. I that needs to take care of me!

Deer Me

By Ironbutt

Well deer season has come around
and Brother Rick and Brother Joe are sure to
take one down.
So off they go to the sportsman store.
Buy bug spray, cammo, bullets and buck lure.
On the way to big hunt place,
Brother Joe found his reading glasses misplaced.
Brother Rick convinced Brother Joe,
aint no big thing that's why we have scopes.
Well they get into the hide and rub that bug juice
on...
but it wasn't really all that long...
before Brother Rick was wondering what's that
smell...
right before they were introduced to hell.
The biggest, meanest buck to be found
came into the hide and was rutting around.
Chased them two boys all through the woods,
finally treed them on Brother Ricks pickup hood.
Now this story has to have an end,
I'll be the one who will do it then.
Seems if a Brother Needs glasses to read,
don't let him hand you a bottle that makes bucks
breed!

Dirt Road Country; Song
By Ironbutt

Daddy built our first house out of four oaks and
some tin.
We worked on it all day long and by night fall we
moved in.
I slept on a dirt floor, wood stove to keep us
warm.
A bucket of tar by the door, in case it would
storm.
I carried out a night pot every day before school.
I am dirt road road country...country old school.
Mama cooked in one pot, everything would go in.
If you did not eat for supper, you'd be sure to see
it again.
I carried water from a pond, so we could take a
bath.
The youngest went in first, the oldest would bath
last.
I carried my little sister on my shoulders when it
rained,
the bus would not run that road until it was dry
again.
Mama died a few years back and I went home on
leave.
That old shack is long gone but those memories
stayed with me.
Like fighting them boys when they cut my hair,
getting a whipping because I ruined school
clothes,

but I got them all back, flat tires don't roll.
County came and told them that old outhouse
would have to go.
They got running water, power and a phone.
I tell folks these stories; they cannot believe it is
true.
I am dirt road country. Country Old School.

Duct Tape on a BMW
By Ironbutt

I work two jobs that take all day,
still the bills pile up that I can't pay.
Today on this road I saw something new....
Duct tape on a BMW!
Hey now that is something new,
duct tape on a BMW.
He aint worried about a drop in class,
that BMW rolls just as fast.
He just became a part of us working class,
he's holding on to that hard earned cash!
I save a few bucks by not buying jeans,
I am in my work clothes longer it seems.
In the park lot of the dollar store,
I saw something a had not seen before.
With a roll of duct tape in plain view,
was a fellow fixing his BMW?
Hey now that's something new,
duct tape on a BMW.
My neighbor and I have slowed down cutting the
grass,
it's eating in to the budget to buy the gas.
Now normally that is not his point of view,
but right now it hides the duct tape on his...
BMW!

Elections

By Ironbutt

Yep I would like to run for a public official,
not that I am politic inclined.
Just want to see what they would dig up, see
what they could find.
Maybe they'd find my old girlfriends, now that
would be so cool.
I could finally get back my jeans and some of my
favorite tools.
Hey they could go looking for some real dirt in the
bars I used to be in.
That wouldn't hurt me in the least bit, be nice to
catch up with old friends.
Course they could go after my Veterans past, see
what I got,
that would leave them explaining a few things
about a No Tell War
but still got shot!
Oh I probably won't get elected, there will be a
scandal or two,
but after all was said and done I bet I could sell a
book or two!

Ever

By Ironbutt

To the heart there is the question, were you ever
here?
Here beside me, my strength, guidance, my love.
The anchor when I needed, the wind to rise above.
The heart has no answer, silent as a stone.
Then I guess the answer to the question would
be....no.
The mind keeps on searching...a void it tries to
cross.
Was there something here, if not, why feel this
loss?
The mind has a suitcase, open and you can see....
there neatly folded, you the memory.
Unfold each one just like a shirt and soon you will
find,
the reason for all the hurt the memory keeps from
the mind.
So no, you were never here, no tender touch ever
shared.
Heart its best we leave it so, hear me and hear me
well.
Memory go back and do your job, we are not
reliving that hell.

Fear

By Ironbutt

The bumper sticker says" No Fear" and I silently
smile inside.
Right!
A smile that offers no delight.
I learned long ago to acknowledge fear in all its
phases,
saw it clear on my men's faces.
Had it shake me to the bones.
Had to deal with on my own.
I have seen fear freeze the strongest man.
Seen fear make people do what others can't.
In the darkest of night or the brightest of days,
fear can walk up on you in so many ways.
Fear of dying, failing or the unknown.
Fear is ever searching for another soul.
So stick your bumper stickers wherever you will,
fear is sitting on your tailgate as you drive over
the hill!

Final

By Ironbutt

Odd.... odd that it seems when things are in the final stage, that departure stage, that it seems to be so good.
Like that last sex before the relationship is over.
Odd.... here I am in front of my troops for the last time.
Spit shine boots, berets. Looking at them as they are looking at me.
Them wanting to be me and me wondering if I could or would do it all again.
Odd.... But then the final salute. The handshake.
The pat on the back and then their new leader, my replacement, gives the command and they move away.
Replacement...Odd.
I watch them leave...slip my beret into my shirt and replace it with my scoot helmet.
Odd...this thing is a lot lighter then that damn old steel pot.
I recover a small brown bag covered bottle from my saddle bags.
Twist the top off... swig to my Brothers who did not get to this day....
put the bottle back into the saddlebags and with a kick on the scoot, head out of the gate.
Past the Welcome to Ft Benning sign and out on to the main road.
Odd....I think that MP just saluted me....Odd
Ironbutt. The Journey

Fireplace Blues

By Ironbutt

The woods been split and had a chance to turn,
brought it in today to see how it will burn.
Got the chores all done and the young ones their
bath,
time to sit in front of this fire and try to relax.
Now of course the cat has got to start purring in
my ear.
There goes the dog swirling on the rug, itching
her rear.
Just get comfortable in that zone;
darn ringing goes off, hey now where is that cell
phone?
Should have filled up my cup
the last time I got up.
Ah, yes now settle back down and just kick back,
you know I think that fire is lack.
Ok so up again and restock this stove,
probably head to bed before I really get it going.
Oh well tomorrow is another day,
just wanted to see if it worked any way.

Friends

By Ironbutt

Had a cardboard box we made into a club house,
hand painted sign said GIRL STAY OUT,
we played in it for hours up on end.
Granny would have hung us high,
if she found out we had lied,
had no clue where her pies had went.
We talked about girls, cars and bikes.
Knew what we hated and what we liked.
Life is easier when you got friends.
Time came and we went off to war.
Lost our youth and maybe more.
Said goodbye to a lot of friends.
I call them up from time to time,
when I hang up I dry my eye.
I wouldn't have made it back without my friends.
Life is easier when you got friends.

Frozen Tears

By Ironbutt

A tour on the frozen DMZ is a year long. A lot can happen in a year. We grow another year older. We lose a year from a relationship. Sometimes we lose that relationship. Among the dangers of the opposing forces there, I feel the casualty list was higher in the lost relationship report. Iron butt; Vet.

I leaned against the orderly room wall and tried to read the letter again.

Man how many weeks I had waited, how few lines were within.

I felt like rushing to a phone and try and talk some sense

but hell this all had already happened...sh.t!

A few of my men walked by...You all right Sarge?

I mumbled a reply back in the dark.

The Korean wind whipped my jacket back and brought me to reality;

I tore the letter up and flushed in the nearest latrine.

5'11 and mean as hell, that's what all the men here will say of me,

so I aint going to let them see a Dear Johns ability.

Open up a Sojou bottle and do a few shots,

take off the boots and crash on the cot.

Tear down my short timers' calendar

and that picture of her.

Put up the picture of the bike of my dreams,
this will take my mind off of her and back on to
the DMZ!

Give Me Wings

By Ironbutt

Daddy give me wings so I can fly.
Do not let my freedom make you cry.
You're the wind beneath my wings.
My new found freedom doesn't change a thing.
Give me freedom so I can fly....
just please be with me when I try.
I've watched my daughter grow,
from the little bundle to the young woman I now
know.
There's a new adventure in the wind,
and they are calling her to join in.
A part of her wants to go,
but she's afraid of leaving me alone.
So I encourage her to fly,
tuck away the tears in my eye.
It will never be a part of me,
to keep a spirit from being free.
So I gave her wings so she could fly.
Her new found freedom made me smile.
She's going to do alright;
I didn't fly so well on my first flight.
Fly high and spread those wings.
See the world and meet new friends.
At the end of the day give your old man a call.
Tell me all about it and what you saw.
Spread your wings and fly, fly, fly....smile

Granny's Saturday Dinner

By Ironbutt

My Granny was one hell of a cook,
no matter what, shot, grown or hooked.
She could add pounds to any man,
what she put together hardly came out of a can.
Now sit down and let me tell you this.
Try staying focus without licking your lips.
She had this way, magic I guess,
the way she'd fry the rabbits we'd get.
Man that woman would be humming around,
baking powder cloud, just a going to town.
That old house would be giving of such a good
smell,
waiting for supper was just agonizing hell.
There would be handmade biscuits and home
grown beans.
A dessert that would make you pops the buttons
on your jeans.
Now don't go ruining that empty place in your
gut,
cause here comes that fried rabbit that will hit
that spot.
Now look at you, you done slobbered on your
chin,
well don't worry none, I saved some in the frig,
here dig right in.
Mean aint I? Smile

Have not Done.

By Ironbutt

There is really not much I have not tried.
Worked hard and try to keep a smile,
but every now and then....
I'd like to scoot across this great land,
what has been defended from jungle to the sands.
Look at a tree line and try not to see,
if that would be a place for the enemy.
Like to see my children not get caught up on
crack,
see them sitting at my table with young ones in
their lap.
Like to look into that woman's eyes,
see us sitting on the porch watching the sunrise.
Yes there are a few things I have not done...
but for now there are these tractors that don't
run.
Smile

Hear Me

By Ironbutt

Hear my cry Brothers of the Silver Wolves, echo
this message for me.
She is out there somewhere, her scent keeps
haunting me.
Be still Laughing Water, mock not my reflection
today.
Heal my inner soul of this torment as your water
washes my face.
See me here my feathered Sister; let me fly with
your magic eyes,
perhaps I can see from up high the place where
my torment lies.
Give me strength powerful Grizzly, I cannot be on
my knees.
Lift me on your strong shoulders, help me to be
free.
Hear me Spirits of the Woods, for today I need the
touch,
I cannot be the traveler alone, my heart is too
heavy, too much.
My peace is needed, the inner soul must heal,
for me to help the Forest, I first must quench this
need.

Heating up the Kitchen
By Ironbutt

Got nothing on but my flannel shirt,
Redneck negligee, in the kitchen hard at work.
Bacon grease behind the ear,
best perfume she can wear.
Hot corn bread, melting butter.
Country style aphrodisiac like no other.
Fixing me a plate with one too many buttons
undone,
bending over and asking me"is everything ok
Hun?"
Got a mouth full of food, need a minute,
got wash these plates if I want any.
So you see there are a lot of chances for romance,
all you need is good cooking and a...

Heroes

By Ironbutt

Daddy what makes a hero, my son suddenly
asked?
We had just watched the parade and the last
soldier pass.
A hero is one that can change the battle fields'
fate,
the actions taken at that moment and the lives it
will save.
Sometimes he gets a hero welcome just like this
parade,
sometimes we honor him alone, we the ones he
saved.

Daddy are you a hero? I had to choke back a tear.
No son I am not but without one I wouldn't be
here.
So son wave high this flag and welcome these
soldiers on,
for somewhere in the back of a plane are flag
covered heroes coming home.

Hey Ironbutt what are You Grilling?

By Ironbutt

Well friends come on in,
doing the finishing touch on this barnyard hen.
Got some apple cider I'm going to let her swim,
got to check the charcoal before I begin.
Got to make sure that flame is nice and low,
going to grill her about an hour or so.
Got some brown sugar that I added a rub,
this hen is going to hit your taste buds.
Sliced up some apples and a mongo or two,
going to put some rice in that left over juice.
Now why don't you just look at this hen,
doesn't it just make you want to dig right in?
Got a little bottle of shine hid under some wood,
why don't you stay for supper, know it's going to
be good!

How Far

By Ironbutt

How far is that Fantasy Land, where chocolate rivers flow?
A land with magic bushes, where gummy bears grow.
Cotton candy colored clouds and lollipop rain.
A place that young and old can visit time and time again.
Well I will tell you but you must listen well, for it is a secret you know.
That magic place is as close to you as you are willing to let your imagination go.
You see with without a little magic, a little bit of hopes and dreams,
this life would be so dark and lonely, a place not to be.
So allow yourselves to let go and splash in a vanilla pond,
bring a plastic cup with you I think the endless soda fountain is already on!

Hymn

By Ironbutt

They were a perfect couple in every way.
Worked hard all week and on Sunday they
prayed.
Walked arm in arm on these troubled shores;
she still left him for a man she loved more.
Oh how he loved that woman, what more can you
say.
She loved him too, fine children she raised.
By his side, lover and a friend,
yet one morning, she still left him.
He had no warning, no note on the bed.
Just a call from the doctor, listened to what he
said.
He shows no anger, no remorse.
The fact that she left him for a man she loved
more.
For the love of that woman, made a foolish man
straight.
He aint out there drinking or running out late.
He works hard all week and on Sunday he prays.
Singing Glory Hallelujah and Amazing Grace.

This is a song I wrote for a friend that suffered
from breast cancer. We lost her too soon.

I am Not an Animal!
By Ironbutt

My head is spinning, the push of the crowd.
I cannot keep my feet, I feel myself going down.
Hands in my pocket. Ripping of my shirt.
Feel the darkness taking over,
reliving the hurt.
Broken, mangled body...impossible on a busy
street.
Yes, this is reality, the final defeat!
I can hear the officers' radio...hear him say no ID.
I find that so ironic, it's always on me?
See the medics coming, wait that's a body bag!
Damn I am not an animal, don't discard me like
that!
So where is this bright shining light? Where is
this eternal peace?
I came home from the land of Hell and this is
what you give to me?
Ok, I have had about enough of this bag and this
damn cold floor.
Give me back my wallet and my keys; I don't want
to hang around here no more.
Hey, hey I said I 'am done here! Why can't you
just let me go?
I hear the sound of silence...then I hear no more.

A tribute; for some the war is never over.

I Can See Her

By Ironbutt

I can just see her stepping off that plane tonight.
Wearing those faded blue jeans.
Ah she'll have that hair pulled back just right,
wearing that perfume that gets to me.
She'll probably know that I have been pacing this
lounge,
carrying that picture she sent to me.
I hope she doesn't know that have sweated on
these palms
and this teddy bear is starting to be a part of me.
I can't wait to hold her, kiss her and then kiss her
again,
can't wait until this distant is gone.
I can't wait, can't wait....can't wait.
Loud speaker says this is the last arrival flight.
There have been two more since the one you
should have been on.
It's just me and this teddy bear here tonight,
guess I saw this all wrong.
There is a teddy bear sitting waiting on a flight....
the flight that you were never on.

I Find Myself

By Ironbutt

I find myself remembering...
the way your hair whipped around your helmet,
not the long braid but the small, loose ones,
the ones that had that keen ability to tickle my
neck
as we scooted down the road.
The way you pressed against me,
trusting.
I find myself remembering....laughing.
I find myself ....handing you that cup of coffee
the morning after, your hair all around you,
confused, waking up in a strange place and
searching my face to
see if I would reveal any information on what had
happened.
I remember you had liked the coffee.
We laughed.
I find myself...now, trying hard to keep those
memories in the right order.
Did I really laugh then? Did you really like the
coffee?
Did we really wake up together?
Was the missing pieces put back together?
Did we really laugh?
I find myself...or do I really?

I Forget

By Ironbutt

I set the table, two forks, spoons and knives.
My nightly ritual, done a thousand times.
Fed the dogs and laundry done.
Every thing the same except for one.
I will eat this meal alone again,
I keep forgetting, not sinking in.
I am not looking across the table at you this time.
No small talk, complements on the meal...left
behind.
Left to pick up the debris of your reckless ways
shattered my world with your presence and still
did not stay.
Demanded so much and yielded not a thing....
I clean up the dishes and empty the sink.
I have not found something to fill in the gap,
nothing ...cleaned up the house, carried out the
trash.
I have refolded my shirts and cut the lawn.
I keep forgetting....you are gone.
Your room stays the same except the clothes
packed away;
you wouldn't come back for them any way.
I finally took your name off my phone;
I have to remember...you're gone.

I Know.

By Ironbutt

I know you're going to leave me; it's just a matter
of time.
I know you're going to leave me, staying gone for
good this time.
You have stopped all your kisses and your hugs
are far apart
but if you're going to leave me you're not taking
my heart.
She's up there in her bedroom and she can hear
ever word.
I know you're trying to hurt me but it's her you
hurt instead.
We have done well without you and we can go on,
so if you're going to leave us you'd best be moving
on.
You've started wearing makeup and stopped
wearing my wedding band,
stopped cooking any supper or treating me like
your man.
You're out there every evening painting the town
and when I come home early, you're nowhere to
be found.
Well I hear you found an other and we've come up
second best,
there is no need in explaining, goodbyes are all
that's left.
I'll take your hand in my hand and shake it like a
friend,

when you walk out that door woman...you're not
welcomed here again!
See I knew you were going to leave me, just a
matter of time.
Knew you were going to leave me, leaving this
entire behind.
Since your hell bent on leaving and tearing us
apart,
just put some dust under that tailgate, you are
not taking my heart!

I Missed It

By Ironbutt

I was seventeen when I left home, bound and
determined
to make it on my own.
Uncle Sam had a plan for me and I took it.
While my buddies had a summer full of fun,
I was learning how to do a parachute jump.
The girls, the beers, I missed it.
That easy road to life I missed it.
There are roads we travel that lead to gold,
mine were dusty with old pot holes.
That easy road to life, I missed it.
At twenty-one I was a man in charge,
married too soon and it fell apart.
I want to ask her for forgiveness but I missed it.
A few more marriages along the way,
a business I could not safe.
I should be rich by now...
but I missed it.
I should have hugged my son the day his team
won.
Told my wife she was the only one.
Finally gave forgiveness to my Mother...
but I missed it.
Some roads will lead you straight to gold;
mine were dusty with old pot holes...
That easy road to life...well....I MISSED IT!

If You Want to Get To Me
By Ironbutt

If you want to get to me....
Feel at ease in a pair of jeans.
Breakfast on the porch with a coffee cup,
making day plans while the sun comes up.
Long hair and soft eyes,
ride on a scoot and love to smile.
If you want to get to me.
Agree to disagree.
Work it out before we go to bed.
Never liked sleeping on wrong words said.
Pull even on the rope of life with me.
Work together to accomplish a dream.
Do not worry when we go out that I am not in the
room,
if you look up you'll see my eyes on you.
Have your fun with all your friends,
at the end of the night we will be together again.
If you want to get to me....
Follow the rose pedals to the bath I ran.
Let me watch you relax and think how lucky I am.
Got no problem helping out with chores,
the sooner we are done, and I can have you more.
Remember that I am a hard working man,
help out with the little things whenever you can.
If you want to get to me....
Wear the perfume that excites my memory.
Smile when ever you open the lunch I made for
you,

a little note of the things I want to do.
If you want to get to me....
it's really not that hard you see.

In The Wind

By Ironbutt

In the wind I can shout the curses I have built up
for you.
The wind dries any tears I have shed for you.
Brother Wind fails me not this night,
many a curses I have and tears to cry.
Fool I was to let you in,
down my shield to be pierced again.
Brother Wind carry what I say,
do not let my curses hurt anyone today.
Dry the tears off my cheek,
disgusted, angry, feel so weak.
Brother Wind, if I may....
Come and blow her memory away.
You are good to me my Brother, thank you friend;
I will try not to call on you so soon again.

In All His Greatness
By Ironbutt

A thought of the day.... not bound by any writing
rule.
The greatest of all birds of wonder...the mighty
eagle.
Wing span, gifted flight, symbol of strength,
courage...
freedom.
Within that mighty birds chest beats a heart, a
heart that keeps
everything it represents functioning.
What if that heart breaks?
Just a thought of the day.

In Your Eyes

By Ironbutt

Sep 24th 2010, Sophie was born...
In your eyes I can plan the future, one step at a time.
Your every minute of life, tiny hands in mine.
Eyes that have not turned into the color you'll claim.
Eyes that have not seen the Worlds struggle or pain.
In your eyes I hope I am the man you will need, guardian, provider, your security.
Your eyes will one day, see the rest of the plan, right now, this moment; see only the reflection of this man.
Welcome to the Journey Sophie, daughter of Brande, granddaughter
of Ironbutt.
Stand tall, live free, be a giver to the needy, respect Life, honor the Dead, take only what you need and never the last one. I whisper in the Wind my prayer for your safe journey.

Inside My Head

By Ironbutt

I think you're getting comfortable, running
around inside my head.
You're moving things around up there, realigning
what's been said.
Oh I don't mind a bit if you decide to stay.
I didn't have much going on up there, at least not
today.
Now I must warn you, listen good as you move
around in there.
There are some things I've tucked away...so just
beware.
If you find a door that does not open, move
around some more.
I'll get back with you one on one and tell you
what's behind that door.
So go ahead make your stay, prop the feet up if
you will.
Welcome to inside my head, you've warmth the
empty chill. Smile

Invisible

By Ironbutt

I am here, here among the living,
see you not me?
You brush past me. I feel the contact.
Therefore I must be real.
I sit. I smell the stench.
I can almost taste the distain you have for me.
I am here, among the living, seeing you not me?
I hear what your thoughts are screaming.
I know what your first impulse is of me.
I was here, here among the living
but I have vanished, this is not where I needed to
be.
Keep moving, rushing, brushing, and crushing.
Deny you needed me.
I was here among the living,
willing to give what I had brought with me.
Hope, Love ... but you were too busy to even see.

IronHorses Riders

By Ironbutt

They ride together or they are seen on their own.
Ironhorse Riders, their origin unknown.
They ride for their freedom, hard earned these
days,
Ironhorse Riders, still letting that flag wave.
Their hair has turned to silver and for some it has
gone away.
They wore a different set of clothes back in their
younger days.
That when they stood together and faced that wall
of steel,
Ironhorse Riders, Brothers forged on bloody
fields.
They take an oath that some would never dare to
keep.
This oath keeps them moving forward longer then
the weak.
No kind of weather can keep the Ironhorse in,
Ironhorse and his Rider, forever in the Wind.
The red, white and blue forever runs through
their veins.
Sleep gets interrupted as they relive that Hell
again.
Those Ironhorse Riders, forever will they say,
Freedom is not free, and it's a Hell of a bill to pay.

Just like Us

By Ironbutt

They wanted men. Men unattached.
Men who had nothing holding them back.
Able to go further and faster than most.
Once signed up, we took an oath.
We worked alone or sometimes in teams.
Few words ever passed between.
We saw the world on Huey skids.
Most folks still don't know what we did.
This was the way, the truth and our lives....
Until that faithful night.
There among the wreckage left behind,
a child, bloody, yet still alive.
Few words spoken but eyes agreed,
we took the child when it was time to leave.
Back at base we named that child;
he became a fire in our lives.
When the missions stopped and our gears was
up.
We gathered around and gave him a hug.
Standing on those Huey skids,
we all waved goodbye to that kid.
We sat in the gun doors, our mission was just,
and we wondered if that kid would grow into us.
Eyes cleared and back on track,
we all took an oath, nothing to hold us back.

Keep It All Together

By Ironbutt

Girl you sure look good to me, on that dance floor
with your moves.
You seem to have it all together, your hair, jeans
and boots.
You aint missed a single step; seem to be right on
time.
I am a man with boots on the ground with only
one thing on my mind.
Can you keep it all together when the world wants
to fall apart?
Can you pull even on that rope when life starts
getting hard?
Will you be in step beside me at the end of the
day?
Can you keep it all together when the music
doesn't play?
I can see you have your standards; you've turned
a few of the boys away.
Buying your own drinks, that says a lot these
days.
There is mud on them cowboy boots, you do more
than dance.
I see you looking at me, is there something you
would like to ask?
Can I keep it all together when the skies start
getting dark?

Will I be the man for you or am I just talk.
Will I be in step beside you at the end of the day?
Can I keep it all together when the music doesn't play?

Leave Us Alone

By Ironbutt

Me and the boys going to make some noise, take
the bikes out for a cruise.
Stop at a bar, lean against the wall and drink a
beer or two.
We aint here for no pick up games, aint taking
anybody home.
We are just here to shake off the week so leave us
alone.
Now we may look like fun to you, leather Romeos,
before you swagger over here there is one thing
you need to know!
Married men. Happy with what we got.
Mother Nature has been good to you and we all
agree you're HOT!
That doesn't mean we are here for you or the
games you play.
So turn around and settle down, please just stay
away!
Just want to lean against the wall, drink a beer or
two.
Not here for anyone and that includes you!

Lesson One:
A Good Hunter Eats What He Catches

By Ironbutt

Something was a eating up all the corn;
we figured it had to be a bear for sure.
So off we went with our coonskin hats and Beebe
guns, cause with the grown folks gone, we sure
figured we had to get this done.
We dug that pit right in the middle of the rows,
had to stand on buckets to get the sand out of
that hole.
We built that bear pit just like on TV,
David Crockett would have been sure proud of my
cousin and me.
We covered up that pit and left that bear a snack,
we covered up our scent and we swished out our
tracks.
That night we all talked about what we would do
with that skin
and then we turned off our lights and off to sleep
we went.
Well the next morning there came on hell of a
shout;
we ran out in our long johns but still had our
guns no doubt.
There in the middle of our trap all hell was
turning loose,
instead of our bear though we had trapped Aunt
Lou!

Now, Uncle, he was a laughing red all in the face,
kept trying to get Aunt Lou out of that place.
She was not having any of that,
we'd get her about half way up and she'd fall right
back.
I'd say it was a quite meeting at the supper table
later that night;
Uncle had taken us out to the barn to set us
right.
I have to give it to that man,
stead of a whipping well, that man shook our
hands!
Said he aint had this much fun with Aunt Lou
since the skinny dipping thing back in 59,
then he stopped and figured we was too young,
maybe some other time.
Smile.

Let the Music Take Me
By Ironbutt

It only takes hearing Angel Flying to Close to the
Ground,
Willy's best and my memories are road bound.
Down to old Ft Benning way, an old smoky bar
called the L& H.
A quarter in the juke box and an eight hour pass,
dancing to a slow one, trying to make the moment
last.
Old Bob Segar and his Turn the Page,
man the memories that song can raise.
An old Ironhead HD, straight kick and me,
sleeping on the ground, cold beer and JD.
Let me hear Freebird by the Lynard Skinner
Band,
I can remember working as a bouncer and getting
stabbed in the hand.
Yep Phil Collins, I Don't Care anymore,
now that was the time I was going through my
divorce.
I'll be Home for Christmas, that one always gets
to me,
heard it played on loud speakers over and over on
the DMZ.
I am sure that when I make my exit and leave this
lives stage,
Garth Brookes the Dance will help end the page.
Smile

Like Me

By Ironbutt

He wanted to be like me,
wear a beret and the Army green.
Asked questions about my battle scars,
the art of war and lands afar.
I told him out of respect,
it's not all glitter, not all that.
For every stripe or every medal,
there is a price and sometimes heavy.
The times I left my loved ones alone,
come back from war and they were gone.
The aches and pains that drain your youth,
never deferred him, he was still going through.
I sit here now folding a flag,
a young man's journey ending in Iraq.
I wonder and worry if this is the pending end,
so many bright faces just like him.
I will carry this ghost until I pass,
had I not deferred him of his task.

Long Line of Veterans
By Ironbutt

My Grandpa was a hell of a man,
WWII and Korean veteran,
when he came home he put a flag up in his yard.
Times were hard but he raised two sons,
I am proud to say my Daddy was one.
I come from a long line of Veterans.
Said the pledge of allegiance every day at school,
brought the flag down when the day was through.
Coach would show us how to fold that flag.
Yes I come from a long line of Veterans.
Hugged my Daddy goodbye under the flag,
it was hard times for us while he was in Nam,
but the good Lord brought him back, just not the
same.
Time came up and I put the uniform on,
jumped out of planes in the early morn,
set a few countries free.
I joined the long line of Veterans just like me.
Yes my Grandpa was a hell of a man!

Lost And Found

By Ironbutt

So a witch left her broom in my tree,
how it got there still puzzles me.
She must not be from around here,
that trees been here for a hundred years.
I climbed up to have a look and see,
not much to the thing to impress me.
Figured I'd at least see some owner tags,
a registration, something so she could get it back.
Walked around to see if I could find
something about her, some kind of sign.
Nothing seems out of place,
guess she's gone without a trace.
Well I'll just leave that broom right on up there
where it's at,
can't really post a Lost and Found ad
Just don't seem right, her leaving her ride
but then again she may have been a FUI
(Flying Under the Influence).
Probably can't remember where she parked that
thing,
has happened to normal folks enjoying too much
drink.
Wonder how you tell someone to pull over on a
broom?
Could she just cast a spell and be sober too?
Oh well, I have had too much candy for one night,
I guess that witch and that broom will be alright.

Love Letter in the Sand
By Ironbutt

I wrote a love letter in the sand, next to the sea.
Bared my ever thought, for your eyes to see.
Each stroke of the stick pronounced my love in
the sand,
as if a painter upon a canvas, brush in hand.
When I was finished, I felt exposed.
What if you don't find this love letter I wrote?
What if a stranger happens by and sees,
this love letter written by me?
Will all my feelings be taken away?
My answer came with the next wave.
Like the painter, I put my brush away,
perhaps what I feel I should not say.

Man in the Mirror

By Ironbutt

There is a man in the mirror looking back at me.
That man in the mirror doesn't like what he sees.
There is a man in the mirror looking back at me.
That man in the mirror...is me.
Got bloodshot eyes and a face that needs to
shave.
A tear on his cheek that seems out of place.
There is this man in the mirror looking back at
me.
That man in the mirror...is me.
Mirror, oh mirror on these empty walls,
how can all of this still fall apart?
After all the compromising and let's try again,
I am left with these empty halls and the sound of
the wind.
Well man in the mirror, I have an idea.
Let's shave that face of yours and get those eyes
clear.
Maybe get a new tattoo to cover up the pain,
go outside and start living again.
There is a man in the mirror looking back at me.
That man in the mirror....is me.

May Need New Parts

By Ironbutt

There's an ad in the paper, yes I put it there,
and some one may read it and respond if they
care.
Free to a good home a slightly used heart.
Yes it still functions but it may need new parts.
Along with this offer comes a pair of strong arms.
Made for heavy lifting but still protect from harm.
Call any hours, or you can text me,
yes this is a real number, yes this is a real deal.
You cannot have any test rides and skeptics stay
gone.
If this doesn't do it, I'd rather stay alone.
Ad said.... May Need New Parts.

Mile Long Grin

By Ironbutt

On the front porch, barefoot, faded overalls and a
baseball cap.
Just a swinging away with a bowl of homemade
ice cream and peaches in my lap.
Talking about trading marbles for a card I haven't
got,
mile long grin on my face,
don't get any better than that.
Carving her name on my favorite climbing tree,
thinking about a kiss, how great that would be.
Holding hands in the pews at church,
eating fried chicken afterwards.
Finally get that kiss and get teased by our friends.
Taking it all with a mile long grin.
Hauling hay until the sun drops from the sky,
gathering up the courage to look her in the eyes.
Reach in my pocket and drop to my knee,
ask her to accept and marry me.
Gather all the kinfolk and play the fiddle loud.
Go find the Preacher and don't daddle around.
Say I do and put on the ring.
Seal with a kiss and a mile long grin!

Music Row

By Ironbutt

Grandpa, all these songs you've written, how
come they aint on the radio?
He was looking through my scrapbooks, I had put
away so long ago.
Well Son I'll tell you, those were dreams I had
when I was young,
life will throw you a curve and other things need
to get done.
There were fields that needed plowing, sure I
wrote down some tunes,
kept them in my overalls but the chores needed
tending to.
I wrote one for your Mother, she liked it even
then,
would singing it to her in the evening while I was
tucking her in.
I wrote one for my Brother, when he passed on us
that June,
brings back fond memories of him when I revisit
that tune.
Had some fancy Nashville man ask me to send
him some,
had high hopes on hearing from him but then
again none.
 Kind of got tired of sending and waiting to hit a
list,
just started writing them down and slowly I guess
I quit.

I saw him read a couple more then he asked if I
would mind,
could he take the book of songs with him and give
it one more try.
My ears are getting old on me and my mind can't
remember
half the time....
Yet to hear one of these songs on the air...well
that would be mighty fine.

Must We Really Now?!

By Ironbutt

The scene of the accident, folks all standing
around.
Everybody's cell phone out, must text this now.
Post this on Facebook got to Tweet my friends.
Someone is reading this text while driving
and BANG...it starts all over again!
Couples don't gaze into each other's eyes
while in a restaurant no they are texting with one
hand, what the hell is wrong?
For a world that objects to invasion of their
privacy,
like the security check for a plane seat,
yet we see more of them then need to see
every time they Tweet!

My Little Girl

By Ironbutt

She is my little girl and will always be....
ah yes those memories.
First there was that Tom boy phase,
soon by make up and perfume replaced.
Bicycles and Barbie skates,
then cars and oh use those brakes!
Oh how priceless the memories....
My little girl and always will be.
Take good care of her Son.

My New Love: A Dedication
By Ironbutt

Your arms reach out for me, still unsure of the
touch.
Your eyes search mine for confirmation,
could there be love this much.
Every day of your being has made it harder to be
apart.
Not one to fall so easily yet I have surrendered to
you my heart.
I make no false predictions, no blind eye to what
lays beyond
I promise only my commitment to be beside you
until you say be gone.
My strength will be your vessel. My love your
guiding star.
My patience there beside you. My wisdom to to
steer from wrong.
Again your arms reach out to hold me, this time I
guide them in.
It is a new found feeling, Love.... Let the new
journey begin.

I dedicate this poem to my new granddaughter
Sophie. Sep 24 2010.

My Uncle

By Ironbutt

He was a big man, comfortable in overall, that's
what you'd find him in.
Firm hand shake and a tobacco stained grin.
Taught me how to sneak like an Injun, cuss like a
sailor,
respect the land and love Mother Nature.
Laughed with us when we locked Aunt Jill in the
smoke house.
Cried with the rest of us when we lost the family
cow.
Even in his sleep, you had to respect the man;
years of hard work left their mark on his hands.
When I told him I was Army bound,
we took our fishing poles to the favorite watering
grounds.
He said, now Son doesn't go being a hero; just get
the job done right.
I taught you how to hunt, shoot and fight.
Don't give any ground and hold that temper back.
Don't tolerate any lazy fools; let them carry their
own packs.
Dig and extra inch our two in that foxhole at
night,
I'll be waiting on you when you get back. It will be
alright.
That was the last talk I had with my Uncle Jim,
he was my hero, a great man. I really, really miss
him.

Name upon A Wall

By Ironbutt

Never was anybody's hero, never caught that
winning ball.
When the boys were picking teams, I'd be the last
they'd call.
So I never thought it would end this way, I gave it
my all....
now I am sitting here with my name upon on a
wall.
We came from different walks of life, different
point of view.
When your life is on the line you don't pick or
choose.
We walked through snow and slept in rain....man
we did it all....
Now we are sitting here with our names upon a
wall.
Farming did not stick to me, packed up and went
away.
Joined the ranks of the men in green, everything
changed.
Seems you can get picked for any thing...man we
did it all...
now we are sitting here with our names upon a
wall.

National Treasure

By Ironbutt

Ever try and find something, something really
needed?
Find darn near everything else, except what
you're seeking.
I needed to find a letter, all legal and all,
I have found enough other things to start my own
mall.
There's that old collector Playboy, I could have
sworn was taken by my son,
I'll have to apologies to him; I got that one all
wrong.
Found the deed to the land, I had to go and file a
new,
hell who knows what I'll find, maybe a dollar or
too. Na.
Found the long lost pacifier, well it was really hid,
man it took a long time for Brande to get over it.
I should show it to her now and see if there's still
a connect,
ok, maybe not I know how touchy pregnant
women get! Smile
so finally I find the letter, man I thought was lost.
So I'll try and see the appointment man, hope this
letter was all.
Smile

Not in this Room

By Ironbutt

The father of my granddaughter now stands at my door.
A trip he has been delaying for a few weeks or more.
I watch him as he hold his daughter, now for the first time.
I can see the transformation, it happens when you hold life.
I leave him for his bonding and my mind goes back years and miles,
far, far away when I held young loves hands in mine.
A young soldier then based in Germany, time for serving my country
and romance was in the air.
It seemed like so long ago, yet I can still hear the laughter after all these years.
The time came short and duty ends, the goodbyes were next in line,
I left that woman alone in a room never knowing I had created life.
Yes there were the could of, should of, didn't do's and I regret each one of them.
My mind creates the ways all over and over, when I let the memories in.
Now it is time for this young man to make a choice on life,
I won't hold a knife to his throat, though the

thought has crossed my mind.
I want him to decide what is the right thing to do;
maybe he won't make the same mistake and leave
a life alone in this room.

Now I Know

By Ironbutt

You won't ever hear me say it much but my Step
Father was a hell of man.
He didn't have to take us in but he made us part
of the plan.
Come home late at night, dead on his feet.
We'd cover him up, untie his shoes, leave him in
his favorite seat.
You see we would all have been throwing always,
if it were not for him.
It took me years to realize, he claimed us all as
kin.
I'm looking now into Times' foggy mirror and can
see what he left behind.
I have the same far away stare and the tired eyes.
I too fall asleep, boots still on my feet.
I wake up in the middle of the night, covered and
in my favorite seat.
Family is everything. Sometimes not all hugs,
but if you let go of this, you let go of Love.

Oh My Son!

By Ironbutt

My quiver lays empty and my tomahawk broken
in two.
The prairie is on fire, our village lies in ruins.
I have seen the fire of hatred that burn in your
eyes,
and that hatred my son...has truly made you
blind.
We watched the wagons coming, the buffalo
disappear.
We fought the white man's bullets with our
arrows and our spears.
I scream from eyes, please take them, for the
white man's words held no truth.
For if the truth were sacred, we would still be
together, three...instead of riding two.

Do not wait until the arrow of truth strikes you
between the eyes to realize the blade of hatred
cuts both ways. Ironbutt.

On Fire

By Ironbutt

Oh Sister of the Lake quenches this fire that rages
through my veins!
Brother Wind please dries these tears that come
from the pain.
My soul is on fire and I see no relieve in sight,
Mother Earth please give me a place to hide.
I have curled up in the arms of Cousin Tree,
told him of my fears and what in my dreams I see.
Nephew Robin listened and tried his best to calm,
yet as I closed my eyes the fire raged on.
Oh Sister of the Lake, is there help here for me?
Let me take a breath and lay here in your arms,
perhaps with your cooling touch, perhaps the
flame will be gone.

On the Lighter Side

By Ironbutt

I was driving down the road,
tired from a hard work day,
when my mind started reading road signs
and went off by it to play.
How long I wonder should I wait for those
Soft Shoulders, Dangerous Curves, Max Height
and of course Max weight?
Then I was alerted by the Blind Driveway,
wouldn't want to run into that!
It was a game my mind enjoyed, so off it went for
another choice.
I should give my bill collectors 90 days since it is
the same as cash.
Oh I wonder if the free beer tomorrow, be actually
today?
Why is it that my jumbo drink only comes with a
regular straw?
If local honey is for sale wouldn't the town folks
talk?
Well I guess I need to get off this Java Alert stuff
cause my mind just goes its way,
I just saw a pizza sign says, Knead dough every
day!

Once

By Ironbutt

Ti's a sad thing when the mind closes down,
that last trick on our life as Death starts his
prowl.
Leaves the body with no warming thoughts,
memories of life lived full of joy and love.
Or perhaps it is not such a tragedy,
a way compassion joins peace of mind in
company.
Yet, here the living still find it a pain,
looking in the eyes of love, never to recall again.

One Bar Left

By Ironbutt

Middle of the night, she is walking down the side
of the road.
Tear smeared makeup and torn clothes.
Through tears she looks at her cell phone, the one
bar is all she has;
help would come...time to call Dad.
She can just hear him rant with what she had
thought was preaching,
realizing now, it was his way of reality teaching.
She shudders at the thought of how he will
unleash his rage,
rage on the man who did this, ruined trust on
what should have been a date.
The wind blows through her torn dress,
yes,
what ever Dad unleashes will finish this.
It's getting colder, she almost slips and falls,
time to end this misery and make the call....
Hello Dad, I know it's late but....
Help was on the way...
someone needs to close Hells Gates!

One Nice Butt

By Ironbutt

I've seen you in here before, along with some of
your friends.
You were a little pricey but I had to see you again.
Each time I came, you were still here but some of
your friends were gone.
I guess there was a party and you didn't go along.
I got a good look at you, the last time I was here.
My mind started wandering what I could do with
you, if I took a care.
So here I am too seeing you and I 'am surprised
that you're alone.
You're just sitting there and all your friends are
gone.
You're not as pricey as you were at first.
You're actually attainable. I hope your feelings are
not hurt.
You don't seem to mind that I run my fingers
across your skin.
You know, I know what I am doing, softly pushing
the tight skin in.
Now, I need to flip you over and look at the other
side.
You have a nice feeling all over and I like your
size.
So, I will take you home and inject you with all of
my special things.
Let you soak until the morning and then the fun
begins.

I'll call a few of my Brothers and they'll all want a view.
They know that I am a master with a butt like you.
By morning the injection will have done their special trick.
I'll start rubbing you down with sweet sensations,
Ah yes baby, this is really rich.
Now by the time we get through playing and I can wash these sticky hands off.
The grill should be seasoned and hot enough, and then baby it's on.
Wrap you up real loose in mango and sweet apples.
Drop a few onions in.
Let you cook for about two hours, and then I'll check on you again.
Man I am glad I found you, we are going to have a great time.
I love BBQing a Butt, especially when it's marked down half price!

Pain Management: Don't get hit

By Ironbutt
Dedicated to 'Big John' 1954-2002

it's time to prep for the nights show,
the band is already unloading at the back door.
Got to brief the new guy and rewalk the floor,
let too many in here the night before.
Use cardboard and tape to protect the ribs.
Shin guards in place for all those low hits.
Take off the jewelry and tie back the hair,
leave nothing for them to grab when you step out
there.
Drink lots of water, swallow a pain pill...
its show time for a bouncer they say is over the
hill.
Crowds looking good for a Saturday night.
Plenty of women, yet somebody will fight.
Seems when not enough space and too much
booze,
messes up the calculation of one and one equals
two!
Got two female bouncers that are a special class
act.
They know how to work it and come in real fast.
Big John gives me the nod and it time to open the
doors.
Lets Rock and Roll baby we are here until four!

* Big John was a bouncer that took me under his wing (a huge wing) taught me to be polite yet forceful. 99% of folks just come to have a good time. It's that 1% that will try to ruin it. That's where we come in.

Red Georgia Clay.

By Ironbutt

Slipping and a sliding trying to make this truck
go.
Holding on the best way I can on this four rut
road.
Groceries flying all over this truck, if I got any
unbroken eggs
it's my day on luck...Stuck!
Slam the door and walk to the house.
Going to be a family affair to get this thing out.
So pull on some boots and pin up your hair.
Somebody push and somebody steer.
Now's there are some rules before we get going.
No stomping on the gas and getting this mud all
throwing.
Nice and easy, not too fast...
if you aint listening you'll end up on your a...s.
So we are a rocking and a pushing, the trucks'
out of there.
Half the young ones got mud in their hair.
Little woman seems to be a little riled up,
Look at my face, it's covered in mud.
"well Honey I read that the rich folks do it all the
time",
besides Darling, that mud suits you just fine!"
* Word of caution* If you aint got a bunch of
young ones already, try a better response then
this.*
you know them rich boys with them big jacked up

trucks.
They spend a lot of money trying to get them
stuck.
I'm thinking that they just got too much time.
Around here dried roads, well they're a lot easier
on the mind!

Redneck Love Token:
Bitter Sweet Results

By Ironbutt

Ah come on Tass!
Roses are red and violets are blue
but they all die in a day or two.
Figured you'd be right touched what I painted on
that barn.
Heck I had to check the spelling, made sure it
wouldn't be wrong.
Now calm down Honey, I did not know for sure
that I had painted the T on a door.
How was I to know with door open when you
passed
that all you think I love is...ss!

Would you like to see your manuscript become a book?

If you are interested in becoming a PublishAmerica author, please submit your manuscript for possible publication to us at:

acquisitions@publishamerica.com

You may also mail in your manuscript to:

**PublishAmerica
PO Box 151
Frederick, MD 21705**

www.publishamerica.com

CPSIA information can be obtained at www.ICGtesting.com
Printed in the USA
LVOW060058050912

297345LV00001B/59/P

9 781456 057176